Also available in this series:
The Cotswolds South
Stratford upon Avon
Oxford
Henley on Thames
Guernsey
Sark
Herm

and shortly to be
followed by:
Bath
Cheltenham
Marlow
The Thames

For information on all
our publications please
see
www.cap-ox.co.uk

The Northern Cotswolds

A little souvenir

CHRIS ANDREWS PUBLICATIONS

Crickley Hill and the view to Gloucester

The Cotswolds

INTRODUCTION

For some the name "Cotswolds" conjures a picture of sheltered valleys harbouring villages of honey coloured stone nestling beside clear, fast flowing streams. Others may see the high, bleak open countryside criss-crossed by dry stone walls, or perhaps the bustling old market towns with their fine perpendicular churches. All these views are united by stone; it is oolitic limestone that has created the underlying landscape of the Cotswolds and the buildings for which the area is famed.

On the western edge of the Cotswold escarpment is the 4000 year old Belas Knap, one of the finest long barrows in the country. Its skilfully constructed dry stone walls are the earliest evidence of stonemasonry in an area known for the quality and hue of its stone.

The Romans established a military zone in the Cotswolds, serviced by routes built with stone, some of those remaining are still followed by today's highways. A grass grown amphitheatre and a museum of Roman treasures remind us of the importance of the market town of Cirencester in former times. The Anglo Saxons left little evidence of their rule, other than a legacy of place-

6 The Market Hall, Chipping Campden

names and a few stone churches tucked away in quiet valleys.

Following the Norman conquest of 1066 the church increased in power and wealth, built upon a thriving wool industry. By Domesday in 1086, most of the present day villages existed and an open field system had been created, with vast flocks of sheep grazing on the open sheep walk.

Today's market towns, such as Chipping Campden and Northleach, were founded at this time, built of local stone with the help of masonry skills brought with the Normans. By the 15th century the whole country was so dependent on the wool industry that the Lord Chancellor's seat in the House of Lords came to be known as the woolsack.

Lower Slaughter

The Cotswolds thrived upon the wool trade; wealthy merchants built fine houses and elegant perpendicular churches. Wool processing became increasingly important to the economy; it was initially a cottage industry, but during the 16th century the weaving and fulling became concentrated in the towns and villages of the western Cotswolds where the fast flowing streams from the steep slopes powered the mills.

Between 1700 and 1840, parliamentary intervention, higher taxation and an increase in wool production elsewhere, led to a decline in the Cotswold wool

industry and the area paid for an over reliance on the trade. Ironically the rich legacy of 15th and 16th century buildings we see today is partly due to this period of poverty, as there was little money available for new building, although a wealthy minority did build several substantial country houses.

The Cotswolds today reflect their interesting and varied past, and the efforts of many to preserve and maintain their atmosphere. The whole area is designated one of Outstanding Natural Beauty and this little book attempts to show something of its charm. This volume shows the area from north to centre, a sister publication "The Cotswolds South" features the centre to the southern edge.

Naunton   11

12 Chipping Campden - Evening procession after Sir Robert Dover's Games

Chipping Campden from the south   13

14   Blockley, south of Chipping Campden, once famouse for its silk mills

Broadway, sometimes described as the 'show village' of the Cotswolds, seen on Christmas Eve

16 Different seasons at: Adlestrop, Chipping Campden,

18   Stanton, an attractive small village, sympathetically restored in the early 1900's

Stanway is another small village but with an impressive Jacobean manor house   19

20   Broadway and the Vale of Evesham from Fish Hill

Lavender at the farm just outside Snowshill 21

22 Snowshill, said to be one of the least altered Cotswold villages

Moreton in Marsh

26   Cotswold life: Sheep and Common Buzzard, hopefully not in conflict

Cattle in fields near Hampnett 27

28   Cotswold bluebells

30   Stow on the Wold, the highest town in the Cotswolds at 800 feet above sea level

The Vicarage at Adlestrop   31

32   The Cotswolds south of Stow

34   Temple Guiting, a village owned and named after the Knights Templar in the twelfth century

36 Winchcombe, once a regional capital of Saxon Mercia

Hailes Abbey, founded 1264 by a son of King John but ruined at the dissolution of the monasteries 37

38   Sudeley Castle with a sculpture by Damien Hurst

Imperial Gardens and The Queens Hotel, Cheltenham

Sunset over fields near Withington 43

44   Gloucester Cathedral, an original Saxon monastery, rebuilt after 1100

46   Upper Slaughter

Lower Slaughter and the nineteenth century corn mill   47

48   Bourton on the Water, sometimes referred to as ' The Venice of the Cotswolds'

50   Great Barrington, Deer Park in winter

Farming is still an important Cotswold industry

52   Charlbury

54   Blenheim Palace, Woodstock in spring

56   Dawn over Cotswold fields near Burford

58   Woodstock, the stocks in Park Street

60   Virginia creeper at Burford, the town often referred to as 'The Gateway to the Cotswolds'

62 Taynton stone was used throughout the Cotswolds as well as at Oxford, Windsor and London

First published 2005

by

Chris Andrews Publications 15 Curtis Yard North Hinksey Lane Oxford OX2 0NA

Telephone: +44(0)1865 723404 email: chris.andrews1@btclick.com. Photos by Chris Andrews, A. Palmer, W.G. Andrews.

Design Chris Andrews and Mike Brain. ISBN 1 905385 03 X All material © Chris Andrews Publications

ISBN 978 1 905385 03 4

www.cap-ox.com

Photos of Blenheim Palace by kind permission of His Grace The Duke of Marlborough

Front Cover: Chipping Campden Title page: Stone carving on Winchcombe Church
This page: Cleeve Hill Back cover: Bourton on the Water